The Book of Quinte Essenqe

or

The Fifth Being.

Early English Text Society
Original Series, No. 16

The Book of Quinte Essence

or

The Fifth Being;

That is to say,

Man's Heaven.

A tretice in englisch breuely drawe out of þe book of quintis e*ss*encijs in latyn, þ*a*t hermys þe p*r*ophete and kyng of Egipt, aft*er* þe flood of Noe fadir of philosophris, hadde by reuelaciou*n* of an aungil of god to him sende.

Edited from
British Museum MS. Sloane 73
about 1460—70 A.D.
by
FREDERICK J. FURNIVALL

Published for
THE EARLY ENGLISH TEXT SOCIETY
by the
OXFORD UNIVERSITY PRESS
LONDON · NEW YORK · TORONTO

OXFORD
UNIVERSITY PRESS

Great Clarendon Street, Oxford OX2 6DP
United Kingdom

Oxford University Press is a department of the University of Oxford.
It furthers the University's objective of excellence in research, scholarship,
and education by publishing worldwide. Oxford is a registered trade mark of
Oxford University Press in the UK and in certain other countries

© The Early English Text Society 1866

The moral rights of the authors have been asserted
Database right Oxford University Press (maker)

First Edition published in 1865
Revised 1889
Reprinted 1965

All rights reserved. No part of this publication may be reproduced,
stored in a retrieval system, or transmitted, in any form or by any means,
without the prior permission in writing of Oxford University Press,
or as expressly permitted by law, or under terms agreed with the appropriate
reprographics rights organization. Enquiries concerning reproduction
outside the scope of the above should be sent to the Rights Department,
Oxford University Press, at the address above

You must not circulate this book in any other form
and you must impose this same condition on any acquirer

Published in the United States of America by Oxford University Press
198 Madison Avenue, New York, NY 10016, United States of America

British Library Cataloguing in Publication Data
Data available

Library of Congress Cataloging in Publication Data
Data available

Original Series, 16

ISBN 978-0-85-991806-0

v

THE odd account of the origin of this Treatise—in its first lines—caught my eye as I was turning over the leaves of the Sloane Manuscript which contains it. I resolved to print it as a specimen of the curious fancies our forefathers believed in (as I suppose) in Natural Science, to go alongside of the equally curious notions they put faith in in matters religious. And this I determined on with no idea of scoffing, or pride in modern wisdom; for I believe that as great fallacies now prevail in both the great branches of knowledge and feeling mentioned, as ever were held by man. Because once held by other men, and specially by older Englishmen, these fancies and notions have, or should have, an interest for all of us; and in this belief, one of them is presented here.

The loss of my sweet, bright, only child, Eena, and other distress, have prevented my getting up any cram on the subject of Quintessence to form a regular Preface. The (translated ?) original of the text is attributed to Hermes—Trismegistus, " or the thrice great Interpreter," so called as "having three parts of the Philosophy of the whole world "[1]—to whom were credited more works than he wrote. The tract appears to be a great fuss about Alcohol or Spirits of Wine; how to make it,

[1] *The Mirror of Alchimy*, composed by the thrice-famous and learned Fryer, Roger Bachon, 1597.

and get more or less tipsy on it, and what wonders it will work, from making old men young, and dying men well, to killing lice.

The reading of the proof with the MS. was done by Mr. Edmund Brock, the Society's most careful and able helper. To Mr. Cockayne I am indebted for the identification of some names of plants, &c.; and to Mr. Gill of University College, London, for some Notes on the Chemistry of the treatise, made at the request of my friend Mr. Moreshwar Atmaram.[1] The Sloane MS. I judge to be about, but after, 1460 A.D.[2] The later copy (Harleian MS. 853, fol. 66) seems late 16th century or early 17th,[2] and has been only collated for a few passages which require elucidation. The pause marks of the MS. and text require to be disregarded occasionally in reading.

EGHAM, 16th *May*, 1866.

P.S. The short side-notes in inverted commas on and after p. 16 (save '5 M^e' and the like) are by a later hand in the MS. The 'Spheres' on p. 26, and the 'Contents,' p. vii-viii, are now added.—F. 1889.

[1] Mr. M. A. Tarkhad has been for many years Vice-Principal of the Rajkumar College, for the sons of the native Chiefs of Rajkote.—1889.
[2] Mr. E. A. Bond of the British Museum has kindly looked at the MSS., and puts the Sloane at 1460-70 A.D., and the Harleian at about 1600.

CONTENTS.

BOOK I.

	PAGE
PROLOG: GOD'S GREATEST SECRET	1
QUINTE ESSENCE DEFINED: ITS QUALITIES	2
HOW TO MAKE QUINTE ESSENCE	4
1ST WAY	4
2ND WAY	5
3RD WAY	5
4TH WAY	5
5TH WAY	6
HOW POOR EVANGELIC MEN MAY GET THE GRACIOUS INFLUENCE OF GOLD	6
HOW TO GILD BURNING WATER OR WINE MORE THOROUGHLY	7
HOW TO MAKE FIRE WITHOUT COALS, LIME, LIGHT, ETC.	8
HOW TO CALCINE GOLD	8
HOW TO SEPARATE GOLD FROM SILVER	9
HOW TO GET ITS QUINTE ESSENCE OUT OF GOLD	9
HOW TO GET ITS QUINTE ESSENCE OUT OF ANTIMONY	10
HOW TO GET ITS QUINTE ESSENCE OUT OF MAN'S BLOOD	11
HOW TO GET ITS QUINTE ESSENCE OUT OF THE 4 ELEMENTS	12
HOW TO FIX ALL EARTHLY THINGS IN OUR QUINTE ESSENCE	13

CONTENTS.

BOOK II.

	PAGE
HOW TO MAKE AN OLD EVANGELIC MAN YOUNG	15
HOW TO CURE A MAN GIVEN UP BY DOCTORS	15
HOW TO CURE THE LEPROSY	16
HOW TO CURE THE PALSY	16
HOW TO FATTEN LEAN AND CONSUMPTIVE MEN	17
HOW TO CURE FRENSY, GOUT, AND TROUBLES FROM DEVILS, WICKED THOUGHTS, ETC., p. 17; AND HOW OUR QUINTE ESSENCE IS HEAVEN	19
HOW TO CURE THE GOUT	19
HOW TO CURE THE ITCH, AND KILL LICE	19
HOW TO CURE QUARTAN FEVER	20
HOW TO CURE CONTINUAL (CHRONIC) FEVER	21
HOW TO CURE TERTIAN FEVER	21
HOW TO CURE DAILY OR QUOTIDIAN FEVER	21
HOW TO CURE AGUE, FEVER, AND LUNACY	22
HOW TO CURE FRENZY AND MADNESS	22
HOW TO CURE CRAMP	22
HOW TO CAST POISON OUT OF A MAN'S BODY	23
HOW TO MAKE A COWARD BOLD AND STRONG	23
HOW TO CURE PESTILENTIAL FEVER	23
HOW THIS QUINTE ESSENCE IS FOR HOLY MEN ONLY ...	25
THE SPHERES AND THE PLANETS	26
MR. GILL'S NOTES ON THE CHEMISTRY OF THE TEXT ...	27
GLOSSARY	29

THE BOOK OF QUINTE ESSENCE

OR THE FIFTH BEING;

THAT IS TO SAY,

MAN'S HEAVEN.

[Sloane MS. 73, fol. 10. Brit. Mus.]

BOOK I.

With þe myȝt, wisdom, & grace of þe holy trynite, I write to ȝou a tretice in englisch breuely drawe out of þe book of quintis essencijs in latyn, þat hermys þe prophete and
4 kyng of Egipt, after the flood of Noe, fadir of philosophris, hadde by reuelacioun of an aungil of god to him sende, þat þe wijsdom and þe science of þis book schulde not perische, but be kept and preserued vnto þe eende of þe world, of alle
8 holy men from al wickid peple and tyrauntis, for greet perilis þat myȝte falle þerof. For wiþinne þis breue tretis, wiþ þe grace of god, I wole more determine of practif* þan of theorik. ȝitt ben boþe nedeful / The firste and souereyneste priuyte þat
12 god, maker of kynde, ordeyned for mannys nede, how þat olde euangelik men, and feble in kynde, myȝte be restorid, and haue aȝen her firste strenkþis of ȝongþe in þe same degree þat is in al kynde, & be mad hool parfiȝtly, except þe strok of þe
16 þundir blast, & violent brusuris, and oppressynge of to myche betynge / Also perilous fallyngis of hiȝ placis, to myche abstynence, & oþere yuel gouernaunce aȝens kynde, And also þe teerme þat is sett of god, þat noman may a-schape, as Iob seiþ in
20 latyn / " Breues dies hominis sunt &c." Forsoþe philosophoris

QUINTE ESSENCE.   B

[Fol. 10.] By the grace of God I translate you this Treatise revealed to Hermes by an angel after Noah's flood, that the knowledge of this book may be preserved to the end of the world.

[* practise, MS. Harl.]

God's greatest secret for man's need is how to restore old feeble men to the strength of their youth,

except in case of thunderblast, and too much fasting, and the term set for all men.

'Nota.'

The purest substance of corruptible things is Quinte Essence or man's heaven.	clepen þe purest substaunce of manye corruptible þingis elementid, 'quinta essencia,' þat is to seie, 'mannys heuene,' drawe out by craft of mani;[1] for whi, as quinta essencia superior, þat is, heuene of oure lord god, in reward of þe .iiij elementis, is 4
[* Fol. 10b.]	yncorruptible & vnchaungeable / riȝt so *quinta essencia su-
Quinte Essence is incorruptible as to the four qualities of man's body,	perior inferior, þat is to seie, mannys heuene, is incorruptible, in reward of þe .4. qualitees of mannys body; and so it is preued naturaly þat oure quinta essencia, þat is, mannes heuene, 8 in it-silf[2] is incorruptible; and so it is not hoot and drie wiþ fier / ne coold and moist wiþ watir / ne hoot & moist with eyr, ne coold and drie wiþ erþe; but oure quinta essencia avayliþ to
but not as the heaven of God.	þe contrarie, as heuene incorruptible / But vndirstonde þat oure 12 qui[n]ta essencia is nouȝt so incorruptible as is heuene of oure lord god; but it is incorruptible in reward of composicioun
It is called, 1. Burning Water; 2. the Soul in the spirit of Wine; 3. Water of Life; and if you wish to conceal it, Quinte Essence.	maad of þe .4. elementis; & it hath .iij. names by the philosophoris, þat is to seie / brennynge watir / þe soule in þe spirit of 16 wyn, & watir of lijf / But whanne ȝe wole concelle it, þanne schal ȝe clepe it 'oure quinta essencia'; for þis name, & þe nature þerof, riȝt fewe philosophoris wolde schewe / but sikurly þei biriede þe truþe with hem. and witiþ weel that it is clepid 20
It is neither moist and cold like water,	brennynge watir; and it is no brennyng watir: forwhi, it is not moist ne coold as comoun watir; for it brenneþ, & so doiþ not
nor hot and moist like air,	comyn watir; ne it is nat hoot and moist as eir, for eir corrumpiþ a þing a-noon, as it schewiþ weel by generacioun of flies, 24 & areins, and siche oþere; but sikirly þis is alwey incorruptible,
nor cold and dry like earth, nor hot and dry like fire.	if it be kept cloos fro fliȝt / Also it is not coold and drie as erþe. for souereynly it worchiþ & chaungiþ. And it is not hoot and drie as fier, as it schewiþ by experience; for hoot þingis it keliþ, 28
It gives incorruptibility,	& hoot sijknessis it doiþ awey / Also þat it ȝeueþ incorruptibi-
[* Fol. 11.]	lite, and kepiþ a þing fro corruptibilite *and rotynge, it is preued
for it prevents dead flesh from rotting,	þus / Forwhi. what pece of fleisch, fisch, or deed brid, be putt þerinne, it schal not corru[m]pe ne rote whilis it is þerinne / 32
and much more the living flesh of man. It is Man's Heaven,	miche more þanne it wole kepe quyk fleisch of mannys body from al manere corruptibilite and rotynge / This is oure quinta essencia, þat is to seie, mannys heuene, þat god made to þe con-

¹ ? MS. meant for 'man.' ² MS. 'siff.'

BOOK I.] THE NATURE AND WORKING OF QUINTE ESSENCE. 3

seruacioun of þe .4. qualitees of mannys body, riȝt as he made
his heuene to þe conseruacioun of al þe world / And wite ȝe for
certeyn þat manye philosophoris and lechis þat ben now, knowe
4 nouȝt þis quinta essencia, ne þe truþe þerof / Forwhi ; god wole
not þat þei knowe it; for her greet brennynge coueitise &
vicious lyuynge / Forsoþe quinta essencia superior, þat is to seie,
heuene of oure lord god bi him silf / Aloone / ȝeueþ not conser-
8 uacioun in þe world, and wondirful influence, but by þe vertue
of þe sunne, planetis, and oþere sterris; riȝt so oure quinta
essencia, þat is, mannys heuene, wole be maad fair wiþ þe sunne
mineralle, fynyd, schynynge, incorruptibile ; and euene in qualite
12 þat fier may not appeire, corrumpe, ne distroie. and þis is verry
gold of þe myn, of þe erþe, or of þe floodis gaderid / for gold of
alkamy maad with corosyues distroieþ kynde, as aristotle and
manye oþere philosophoris prouen / and þerfore good gold na-
16 turel, & of þe myn of þe erþe, is clepid of philosophoris 'sol' in
latyn ; for he is þe sonne of oure heuene, lich as sol þe planet is
in þe heuene aboue ; for þis planete ȝeueþ to gold his influence,
nature, colour, & a substaunce incorruptible. And oure quinta
20 essencia, mannys heuene, is of þe nature *& þe colour of heuene /
And oure sol, þat is, fyn gold of þe myne, schal make it fair, riȝt
as sol þe planete makiþ heuene fair / and so þese two togidere
ioyned schal ȝeue influence in us, and þe condiciouns of heuene
24 and of heuenly sonne / in as miche as it is possible in deedly
nature, conseruacioun and restorynge of nature lost, & renew-
ynge of ȝongþe / And it schal ȝeue plenteuously heelþe: and so it
is preued by astronomy aboue, þat steŕris þat haþ influence vpon
28 þe heed and þe necke of man / as ben þe sterris of aries, taurus,
and gemini, ȝeuen influence syngulerly vpoñ Gerapigra galieni /
And þerfore it haþ a synguler strenkþe, by þe ordynaunce of
god, to drawe awey þe superflue humouris fro þe heed, þe necke,
32 and þe brest, and not fro þe membris byneþe / And so I seie of
spicis þat drawiþ humouris fro þe knees, þe leggis, and þe feet,
þat resseyuen a synguler influence of þe sterris of Capricorn,
Aquarie and pisces, & riȝt so of oþere, et cetera / Comounne
36 ȝe not þis book of deuyne secretes to wickid men and auerous ;

[Side notes:]
preseruyng his body as Heauen does the world.
Many know it not now for their covet- ousness and vice.
But as God's Heaven is aided by sun and stars, so our Heaven, or Quinte Essence, is made fair by the sun mine- ral, or pure gold of the mine, not of alchemy.
'Nota.'
Good natural gold is called Sol, because Sol the planet gives gold its power, colour, &c.
Our Quinte Essence is the [* Fol. 1b.] colour of hea- ven; gold makes it fair; and the two work in us (so far as is pos- sible) renewal of youth, and give health plenteously.
As Aries, Taurus, and Gemini draw humours from the head and breast,
'Nota.'
and not the limbs be- neath, so those spices that do draw from these limbs get their power from Capri- corn, &c.
Tell not these Divine secrets to wicked men.

THE 1ST WAY TO MAKE QUINTE ESSENCE. [BOOK I.

Marginalia:
- 'aqua vite'
- *To make Quinte Essence.*
- Take the best wine, or any not sour; distil it, and the 4 Elements shall be left like dregs. Distil 7 times to get Burning Water;
- [* Fol. 12.]
- put this in a Distiller in a furnace, and 'vas' let the vapour rise, condense, and be distilled till it is turned into Quinte Essence, and parted from the 4 elements.
- 'Nota.'
- Distil it 1000 times, and it shall be glorified and become a medicine incorruptible as heaven.
- After many days unstop your distiller,
- 'lute'
- and if there issues out a heaven-sweet savour, you
- [* Fol. 12*b*.] have our Quinte Essence. If not, distil again till you have.

but kepe ȝe it in priuytee / Take þe beste wiyn þat ȝe may fynde, if ȝe be of power; & if ȝe be riȝt pore, þanne take corrupt wiyn, þat is, rotyn, of a watery humour, but not egre, þat is, sour, for þe quint essencia þerof is naturaly incorruptible 4 þe which ȝe schal drawe out by sublymacioun / And þanne schal þer leue in þe ground of þe vessel þe .4. clementis, as it were, rotun fecis of wiyn / But firste ȝe muste distille þis wiyn .7. tymes; & þanne haue ȝe good brennynge watir / Forsoþe, 8 þis is þe watri mater *fro which is drawe oure quinta essencia / Thanne muste ȝe do make in þe furneis of aischin, a distillatorie of glas al hool of oo. pece, wiþ an hoole a-boue in þe heed, where þe watir schal be putt yn, and be take out / And þis is a 12 wondirful instrument þat þat þing þat by vertues of fier ascendith and distillith wiþinne þe vessel, per canales brachiales, þat is, by pipis lich to armys, be bore aȝen, and eftsoones ascendith, & eft descendiþ contynuely day and nyȝt, til þe brennynge water 16 heuenly be turned into quintam essenciam / And so bi continuelle ascenciouns & discenciouns, þe quinta essencia is departid fro þe corruptible composicioun of þe .4. elementis. For bifore þat þing þat is twies sublymed is more glorified, and 20 is more sotil, and fer from þe corrumpcioun of þe .4. elementis more separat þan whanne it ascendith but oonys; and so vnto a þousand tymes, so þat by contynuel ascendynge and descendynge, by the which it is sublymed to so myche hiȝnes of glorifi- 24 cacioun, it schal come þat it schal be a medicyn incorruptible almoost as heuene aboue, and of þe nature of heuene / And þerfore oure quinta essencia worþily is clepid 'mannys heuene' / And aftir manye daies þat it hath be in þis sotil vessel of glas 28 distillid / ȝe schulen opene þe hoole of þe vessel in þe heed þat was selid with þe seel of lute of wijsdom, maad of þe sotillest flour, and of white of eyren, and of moist papere, ymeyngid so þat no þing respire out / And whane ȝe opene þe hoole. if þer 32 come out a passynge heuenly swete flauour þat alle men þat come yn naturely *drawe þerto. þanne ȝe haue oure quinta essencia / and ellis sele þe vessel, and putte it to þe fier aȝen til ȝe haue it. 36

[Book I.] THE 2ND, 3RD, AND 4TH WAYS OF MAKING QUINTE ESSENCE. 5

And anoþer maner worchinge of oure quinta essencia is
þis / Take þe noblest and þe strengest brennynge watir þat ʒe
may haue distillid out of pure myʒty wiyn, and putte it into
4 a glas clepid amphora, with a long necke / and close þe mouþ
strongly wiþ wex; And loke þat half or þe þridde part be fulle;
and birie it al in hors dounge, preparate as it is seid hereafter /
so þat þe necke of þe glas be turned dounward, & þe botum
8 be turned vpward, þat by vertu of þe hors dounge þe quinta
essencia ascende vp to þe botum. And þe grosté of þe mater
of þe watir descende dounward to þe necke / And aftir manye
daies, whanne ʒe take it out, softly lift vp þe glas as it stondith,
12 and ʒe schal se in þickenes and cleernesse a difference bitwene
þe quintam essenciam sublymed, and þe grose mater þat is in þe
necke / þe wondirful maistry of departynge of þat oon fro þat
oþer is þis / Take a scharp poyntel, or a pricke of yren, &
16 peerse into þe wex þat hongiþ in þe mouþ of þe glas aʒens þe
erþe / and whanne ʒe haue peersid al fully to þe watir, take out
þe poyntel or þe pricke / And þat erþely watir wole first come
out þat is in þe necke / and so til it be come out vnto þe
20 departinge bitwixe it / and þe quinte essence, þat is, mannys
heuene sublymed. and whane ʒe se þat þis quint essence wole
renne & melte aftir þat þis erþely watir be voydid, putte þanne
swiftly ʒoure fyngir to þe hoole, & turne vp þe glas, and þanne
24 ʒe haue þerinne oure quinte essence, *and þe erþely watir wiþoute
aside. And þis is a passyng souereyn priuytee.

The þridde maner is, þat ʒe take a greet glas clepid amphora,
and seele it weel, and birie it weel in þe wombe of an hors al
28 togidere. and þe pureté of þe quinte essencie schal be sublymed
aboue, & þe grosté schal abide byneþe in þe botme / take out
softli þat þat fletiþ a-boue; and þat þat leeueþ bihynde, putte it
to þe fier.

32 The .iiij. maner is þis. take what vessel of glas þat ʒe wole,
or of erþe strongly glasid, and þer-vpon a round foot of glas
wiþ a leg. and seele þe vessel with his couertour, þat þe rod
of þe foot of þe glas wiþinne þe vessel honge in þe eyr, þat þat
36 þing þat ascendith to þe couertour in þe maner of a pott boilynge

The second way to make Quinte Essence.

Put the strongest Burning Water into an 'amphora;' seal it up; bury it neck downwards in horse-dung, and the Quinte Essence will rise into the globe and the impurities settle in the neck.

Take the glass out of the dung;

make a hole in the wax seal,

let out the impure earthly water,

and when the Quinte Essence would begin to run, turn the glass up, and keep

[* Fol. 13.]

your Quinte Essence.

The third way.

Put your amphora into a horse's belly instead of the dung, and proceed as above.

The fourth way.

Substitute for the amphora a vessel of glass or earth, with a tube running from the top and hanging in the air,

The fifth way. Distil your Burning Water ten times.	descende doun aȝen by þe foot of þe glas. and this instrument may ȝe do make wiþoute greet cost / The fifþe maner is, þat þe brennynge water be .10 tymes distillid in hors dounge contynuely digest.

into which the vapour may fall and condense.

descende doun aȝen by þe foot of þe glas. and this instrument may ȝe do make wiþoute greet cost / The fifþe maner is, þat þe

The fifth way.

brennynge water be .10 tymes distillid in hors dounge con-

Distil your Burning Water ten times.

tynuely digest. 4

To make fire without fire, and Quinte Essence without cost or trouble.

The science of makynge of fier wiþoute fier / wherby ȝe may make oure quinte essence wiþoute cost or traueile, and withoute occupacioun and lesynge of tyme / Take þe beste horse dounge þat may be had þat is weel digest, and putte it wiþine 8

Put horsedung into a vessel or pit lined with ashes, and place your vessel in it up to the middle. The cold top part will condense the vapour caused by the heat of the dung.

a uessel, or ellis a pitt maad wiþ þe erþe anoyntid þoruȝout with past maad of aischin. And in þis vessel or pitt, bete weel togidere þe dounge; And in þe myddil of þis doung, sette þe vessel of distillacioun vnto þe myddis or more / For it is nede þat al þe 12 heed of þe vessel be in þe coold eir / þat, þat þing þat bi vertu of þe fier of þe doung þat ascendith þerby be turned into watir

[* Fol. 13b.]

*by vertu of cooldnes of þe eir and falle doun aȝen and ascende vp aȝen. and þus ȝe haue fier wiþoute fier, and but wiþ litil 16 traueile.

Or, place your vessel in the sun's rays.

Also anoþer maner of fier. sette ȝoure vessel forseid to þe strong reuerberacioun of þe sunne in somer tyme, and lete it stonde þere nyȝt and day. 20

How poor evangelic men may get the gracious influence of gold.

Here I wole teche ȝou how pore euangelik men may haue wiþoute cost, and almoost for nouȝt, þe gracious influence of gold, and þe maner of þe fixynge of it in oure heuene, þat is,

Borrow a Florence florin of a rich friend, anneal [? heat] it on a plate of iron, and throw it into some Burning Water, taking care to quench the fire quickly to prevent the Water wasting.

oure quinta essencia. if ȝe be pore, ȝe schal preie a riche man 24 þat is ȝoure freend to leene ȝou a good floreyn of florence / and anele it vpon a plate of yren as yren is anelid. and haue biside ȝou a uessel of erþe glasid, fillid ful of the beste brennynge watir þat ȝe may fynde. & caste into þe watir þe floreyn anelid. and 28 loke þat ȝe haue a sotilte and a sleiȝþe to quenche sodeynly þe fier, þat þe watir waaste not ; and be weel war þat non yren touche

Repeat this 50 times

þe watir. but aff[t]er caste into þe watir þe floreyn, and do so .l. tymes or more, for þe oftere þe bettere it is / And if ȝe se þat þe 32

in fresh Water, and then mix all the Waters together.

watir waaste to myche, chaunge it þanne, and take newe, & do so ofte tymes. and whanne ȝe haue do ȝoure quenchour, putte alle þe watris togidere / And ȝe schulen vndirstonde þat þe

The Water draws out all

vertu of brennynge watir is sich þat naturely it drawiþ out of 36

BOOK I.] HOW TO GILD BURNING WATER OR WINE. 7

gold alle þe vertues & propirtees of it, & it holdiþ incor- *the properties of the gold.*
rumptibiletee & an euene heete. *þanne meynge þis brennynge [* Fol. 14.]
watir þus giltid wiþ oure quinte essence, and vse it. but be war *Mix the gilt Burning Water with Quinte Essence.*
4 þat ȝe quenche not þe floreyn in oure quinte essence; for þanne
it were lost / And if it so be þat ȝe haue not þis brennynge watir *You may substitute for Burning Water best white wine, which also retains the powers of gold.*
redy, þanne quenche ȝoure floreyn in þe beste whiȝt wiyn þat
may be had / For sikirly þe philosophore seiþ, þat wiyn hath
8 also þe propirtee to restreyne in it þe influence and vertues of
gold / And whanne ȝe haue do ȝoure werk, ȝe schal wite þat þe
floreyn is als good, & almoost of þe same weiȝte, as it was
afore / þerfore vse wiyn or brennynge watir giltid, so þat ȝe may *This gilt Water will make you well and young again. In it you have the Sun fixed in our Heaven.*
12 be hool, and wexe glad, and be ȝong. And þus ȝe haue oure
heuene, and þe sunne in him fixid, to þe conseruacioun of mannys
nature and fixacioun of oure heuene, þat is, oure quinte
essence.

16 The science how ȝe schule gilde more myȝtily by brennynge *'science.'*
watir or wiyn þan I tauȝte you tofore, wherby þe water or *How to gild Burning Water or Wine more thoroughly.*
þe wiyn schal take to it myȝtily þe influence & þe vertues
of fyne gold.

20 Take þe calx of fyn gold as it is declarid here-aftir in þis *Heat calcined gold in a silver spoon and put it in Burning Water or wine 50 times, as with the florin before. Your liquor will be better gilt, as the fire and Water or [* Fol. 14b.] wine work more powerfully on the grains of gold than on a plate. Wine retains the properties of all liquibles quenched in it. If Saturn (lead) liquefied be quenched in wine, and then Mars (iron) be quenched in it, Mars acquires the softness of Saturn.*
book, and putte it in a siluer spone, and anele it at þe fier.
& þanne caste þe cals of the gold in þe brennynge watir
or in wiyn .l. tymes, as I tauȝte ȝou tofore wiþ þe floreyn. and
24 ȝe schule haue ȝoure licour by an hundrid part bettir gilt þan ȝe
had tofore wiþ þe floreyn / Forwhi. fier worchiþ more strongly
and bettere *in sotil parties þan it doiþ in an hool plate / And
also brennynge watir or wiyn drawiþ out more myȝtily bi a
28 þousand part þe propirtees of gold fro smale parties anelid, þan
it doiþ fro a þicke plate / And ȝe schal vndirstonde þat wiyn
not aloonly holdiþ in it þe propirtees of gold, but myche more
þe propirtees of alle liquibles if þei be quenchid þerinne. and þat
32 is a souereyn priuite: Forwhi, if ȝe quenche saturne liquified
in wiyn or in comoun watir .7. tymes, and aftirward in þat wiyn
or watir ȝe quenche mars manye tymes, þanne mars schal take
algate þe neischede and þe softnes of saturne / And þe same
36 schal venus do, & alle opere liquibles / or ellis, And ȝe

8   TO MAKE FIRE WITH NO FIRE. TO CALCINE GOLD. [Book I.

Again, if you quench Mars in wine and put in it Saturn liquefied, this will be made hard.

quenche mars in whiʒt wiyn or in comoun watir manye tymes, and aftirward in þe same wiyn or watir ʒe caste saturne liquified ofte tymes, þanne wiþoute doute ʒe schal fynde þat þe saturne is maad riʒt hard / Therfore þe propirtees of alle liquibles may 4 be brouʒt into wiyn or watir; but myche more myʒtily into brennynge watir good and precious.

To make fire without coals, lime, light, &c.

The science to make a fier, þat is, wiþoute cole, wiþoute lyme, wiþoute liʒt, worchinge aʒens al maner scharpnes or 8 accioun of visible fier, riʒt as worchiþ þe fier of helle / And þis priuytee is so vertuous, þat þe vertu þerof may not al be declarid. And þus it is maad. Take Mercurie þat is sublymed

Mix equal parts of sublimated Mercury, Salt, and Sal Ammoniac, grind them small, expose them to the air, and they'll turn into water,

[* Fol. 15.] wiþ vitriol, *& comen salt, & sal armoniac .7. or .10. tymes 12 sublymed / and meynge hem togidere by euene porcioun. and grynde it smal, and leye it abrood vpon a marbil stoon; and by nyʒte sette it in a soft cleer eir, or ellis in a coold seler; and þere it wole turne into watir / And þanne gadere it togidere in to 16 a strong vessel of glas, and kepe it / This water forsoþe is so strong, þat if a litil drope þerof falle vpon ʒoure hond, anoon it

a drop of which will eat thro' your hand, and make Venus (copper) or Jupiter (tin) like pearl. If it could be moderated it would cure the disease Hell fire, and every corrosive sickness.

wole perce it þoruʒ-out; and in þe same maner it wole do, if it falle vpon a plate of venus or Iubiter, into þis watir, it turneþ 20 hem into lijknes of peerl. who so coude reparale & preparate kyndely þis fier, wiþoute doute it wolde quenche anoon a brennynge sijknes clepid þe fier of helle. And also it wolde heele euery cor[os]if sijknesse. And manye philosophoris clepiþ þis 24

'sal amarus.' It is also called 'Sal Amarus.'

þing in her bookis 'sal amarus,' al þouʒ þei teche not þe maistrie þerof / If it be so þat þis firy watir breke þe glas, and renne out into þe aischen, þanne gadere alle togidere þat ʒe fynde pastid in þe aischen / and leye it vpon a marbil stoon as afore, and it wole 28

'Science.' To calcine gold.

turne into watir. And þis is a greet priuytee.

The science to brynge gold into calx / Take fyn gold, and

Cut gold into shavings; put it into a crucible with Mercury; heat it, and it will crumble [Fol. 15b.] into dust like flour. Heat it more till the mercury goes his way;*

make it into smal lymayl: take a crusible wiþ a good quantitee of Mercurie, and sette it to a litil fier so þat it vapoure 32 not, and putte þerinne þi lymail of gold, and stire it weel togidere / & aftirward *wiþinne a litil tyme ʒe schal se al þe gold wiþinne þe Mercurie turned into erþe as sotil as flour. Þanne ʒeue it a good fier, þat þe Mercurie arise and go his wey; or ellis, 36

BOOK I.] TO GET THE QUINTE ESSENCE OUT OF GOLD.   9

and ȝe wole, ȝe may distille and gadere it, puttynge þer-vpon a *or distil it, and the gold powder will be in the crucible.*
lembike / and in þe corusible ȝe schal fynde þe gold calcyned and
reducid into erþe / And if ȝe wole not make lymayl of gold,
4 þanne make þerof a sotil þinne plate, as ȝe kan, and putte wiþinne *A thin plate of gold will do instead of shavings, and*
þe Mercurie al warm; and ȝe schal haue ȝoure desier / And *Silver may be treated like gold.*
in þis same maner ȝe may worche wiþ siluir / Thanne take þe
calx of þese two bodies, and bere hem openly wiþ ȝou; and þer *To carry these powders*
8 schal noman knowe what þei ben / And if ȝe wole bere hem *about,*
more priuyly wiþoute ony knowynge, þanne meynge hem wiþ *mix them with pitch,*
pich melt, or wex, or ellis gumme, for þanne noman schal knowe *wax, or gum,*
it what it is. And whanne ȝe wole dissolue ony of þese calues *melting the mass when*
12 by hem silf, putte eiþir by him silf in a test, or ellis þe pich or *you want the metal.*
þe wex in which þei ben ynne; and anoon schal come out verry
gold & siluer as þei were tofore.

Now I wole teche ȝou þe maistrie of departynge of gold *How to separate gold*
16 fro siluir whanne þei be meyngid togidere / Forsoþe ȝe woot *from siluer when mixed with it.*
weel þat þer be manye werkis in þe whiche gold and siluir
be meyngid, as in giltynge of vessel & Iewellis / þerfore *Put the mixture into a*
whanne ȝe wole drawe þe toon fro þat oþir, putte al þat mixture *solution of vitriol and*
20 into a strong watir maad of vitriol and of sat petre. and þe *saltpetre, and the silver will be dissolved.*
* siluyr wole be dissolued, and not þe gold: þanne ȝe haue þat *[* Fol. 16.]*
oon departid fro þe toþir / And if ȝe wole dissolue þe gold to *Corrosive*
watir, putte þanne yn þe watir corosyue, Sat armoniac; and þat *water and sal ammoniac will dissolve*
24 watir wiþoute doute wole dissolue gold into watir. *the gold.*

The science to drawe out of fyn gold v^{ta} essencia is þis / *'science.' 'Nota.'*
First ȝe schal reduce gold into calx, as I tolde ȝou tofore / *How to get out of gold its*
þanne take vynegre distillid, or ellis oold vryne depurid fro þe *Quinte Essence.*
28 fecis, and putte it in a uessel glasid; and þe liquor schal be in
þe heiȝþe of 4. ynchis; and þerinne caste þe calx of gold, & *Put calcined gold into distilled vinegar or purified urine; set it*
sette it to the strong sunne in somer tyme, þere to abide / and *in a hot sun;*
soone aftir ȝe schal se as it were a liquor of oyle ascende vp, *a film will*
32 fletynge aboue in maner of a skyn or of a reme. gadere þat awey *soon rise; skim it off,*
wiþ a sotil spone or ellis a feþere, and putte it into a uessel of *collect all such in a*
glas in þe which be putt watir tofore. and þus gadere it manye *glass vessel till no more*
tymes in þe day, into þe tyme þat þer ascende nomore / and aftir *rise. Evaporate*
36 do vapoure awey þe watir at þe fier. And þe v^{ta} essencia of þe *the water left; the residuum*

C

TO GET THE QUINTE ESSENCE OUT OF ANTIMONY, &C. [Book I.

is the Quinte Essence of Gold.
[¹ then, MS. Harl.]
And if you fix this Quinte Essence in our heaven, it will restore man to the strength of his youth.
[* Fol. 16b.]
Now I have [Nota.] *told this most sovereign secret, which should not be shewed. The Quinte Essence of gold is best to heal wounds.*

gold wole abyde byneþe. And manye philosophoris clepiþ þis quinta essencia an oile incombustible, þat is a greet priuytee / And if ȝe wole fixe þis quinta essencia in oure heuene, þat¹ it may wiþoute doute restore aȝen to man þat nature þat is lost, 4 and reduce him aȝen into þe vertu of þe strenkþe of ȝongþe, and also lenkþiþ his lijf into þe laste terme of lijf set of god // Now forsoþe I haue toold ȝou þe souereynest *priuytee and restorynge of mannys kynde, and in part greet þing þat schulde not be 8 schewid / Forwhi. þis oyle, þat is to seie, quinta essencia of gold, hath þe mooste swetnes and vertu to a-swage and putte awei þe ache of woundis, and for to heele woundis, oolde sooris, and manye wondirful yuelis / Also in þe same maner ȝe may drawe 12 out of siluir, quinte essencie //

How to get its Quinte Essence out of Antimony.

Put powdered antimony into distilled vinegar; heat it till the vinegar is red; take away the red vinegar, and put fresh; take that away when red. Put the red vinegar into a distiller, and 1000 drops of blessed wine shall come down the pipe; collect this; it is an incomparable treasure.

The science to drawe out of antymony, þat is, mercasite of leed, þe vᵗᵉ essencie, is a souereyn maistrie, and a priuytee of alle priuytees / Take þe myn of antymony aforeseid, 16 and make þerof al so sotil a poudre as ȝe kan / þanne take þe beste vynegre distillid, and putte þerinne þe poudre of antymonye, and lete it stonde in a glas vpon a litil fier into þe tyme þat þe vynegre be colourid reed. þanne take þat 20 vynegre awey, and kepe it clene, and putte aȝen þer-to of oþere vynegre distillid, and lete it stonde vpon a soft fier til it be colourid reed. & so do ofte tymes. and whanne ȝe haue gaderid al ȝoure vynegre colourid, putte it þanne in a distillatorie. and 24 first þe vynegre wole ascende ; þanne after ȝe schal se merueilis : for ȝe schal se as it were a þousand dropis of blessid wiyn discende doun in maner of reed dropis, as it were blood, by þe pipe of þe lymbike / þe which licour, gadere togidere in a 28 rotumbe / and þanne ȝe haue a þing þat al þe tresour of þe world

[Nota.]
[* Fol. 17.]
It cures the pain of all wounds,

and when fermented it works great secrets.

may not be in comparisoun of worþines þerto / aristotle seiþ þat it is his lede in þe book of secretis, al þouȝ he *telle not þe name of þe antymonye aforseid / Forsoþe þis doiþ awey ache of alle 32 woundis, and wondirfully heeliþ. þe vertu þerof is incorruptible & merueilous profitable / it nedit to be putrified in a rotombe and seelid in fyme, and þanne it worchiþ greet priuytees / Forsoþe þe vᵗᵃ essencia of þis antymony þat is reed, in þe which is 36

BOOK I.] TO EXTRACT THE QUINTE ESSENCE FROM MAN'S BLOOD.

þe secreet of alle secretis, is swettere þan ony hony, or sugre, or ony oþir þing.

The science in the extraccioun of þe .5[1] essencie from blood, and fleisch, & eggis / To ȝou I seie, þat in every elementid þing, þe .5. essencie remayneþ incorrupte: it schal be þanne þe moost þing of merueyle if I teche ȝou to drawe out þat fro mannys blood reserued of Barbouris whanne þei lete blood; also fro fleisch of alle brute beestis, and fro alle eggis, and oþere suche þingis. for als myche as mannes blood is þe perfitist werk of kynde in us, as to þe encrees of þat þat is lost, it is certeyn þat nature þat .5. essence maad so perfiȝt þat, wiþoute ony oþir greet preparacioun wiþoute þe veynes, it beriþ forþ þat blood anoon aftir into fleisch. and þis 5 essence is so nyȝ kynde þat [it] is moost to haue[2] / Forwhy. in it is merueylous vertu of oure heuene sterrid, and to þe cure of nature of man worchiþ moost deuyn myraclis, as wiþinne I schal teche ȝou / þerfore resceyue of Barbouris, of ȝong sangueyn men, or colerik men, whanne þei be late blood, þe which vse good wynes. take þat blood aftir þat it haþ reste, and cast awey þe watir fro it, and braie it wiþ þe .10. part of comen salt preparate to medicyns of men; and putte it into a uessel of glas clepid amphora, þe which, sotely seele, and putte it wiþinne þe *wombe of an hors, preparate as tofore, and renewe þe fyme oonys in þe wike, or more, and lete it putrifie til al þe blood be turned into watir / and it schal be doon at þe mooste in xxx. or xl dayes, or aftir, more or lasse / þanne putte it in a lembike, and distille it at a good fier / what so euere may ascende, putte þat watir vpon þe fecis brayed, meyngynge vpon a marbil stoon; putte it aȝen, and aftir distille it aȝen manye tymes rehersynge / And whanne ȝe haue þis noble þing of blood, þerof þe .5. beynge drawe out / putte aȝen þe watir in þe stillatorie of circulacioun til ȝe brynge it to so myche swetnes & an heuenly sauour, as ȝe dide þe brennynge watir. and þis is þe 5 beynge of blood deuyn, and miraclis more þan man mai bileue but if he se it.

Science.

How to get its Quinte Essence from Man's Blood.

Man's blood is the perfectest work of nature in us, and its Quinte Essence converts blood into flesh,

*and works divine miracles of healing. Get from Barbers the blood of young sanguine men; let it stand; pour off the serum; mix the blood with a tenth of prepared salt; put it in an amphora; seal that up; put it in a horse's belly, [*Fol. 17b.] renewing the dung weekly till all the blood turns into water; distil that; put the outcome on the pounded fæces, and distil over again.*

Heat the water in the distiller till it comes to a heavenly savour. This Fifth Being works miracles hardly credible unless seen.

---

[1] 5 for *fifth*, or *quinte*.
[2] MS. Harl. reads 'and this fifte beinge so nighe kinde it is most to haue.'

To get the Quinte Essence out of capons, beasts, eggs, &c.

Grind some of them with a tenth part of prepared salt; put 'em into a horse's belly till they become water, and distil that till it's heaven-sweet.

Now wole I· teche ȝou to drawe out þe .5 beynge from capouns, hennes, and al maner fleisch of Brut beestis, and from al maner eggis of foulis þat ben holsum and medicynable to ete for man kynde / Grynde summe of þese þingis 4 forseid, which þat ȝe wil, as strongly as ȝe can in a morter, wiþ þe 10 part of him of sal comen preparate to þe medicyne of men, as I seide tofore. putte it in þe wombe of an hors til it be turned into water. distille as it is aforeseid, and in þe stillatorie 8 of circulacioun þe watir þat is distillid, putte it in aȝen til it be brouȝt to þe swete heuenly sauour and smel aforeseid /

'science.'

To draw the Fifth Being out of each of the Four Elements, and to separate them.

The science to drawe out þe 5 beynge of euerych of þe .4 elementis, and to schewe euerych of þe forseid þing bi hem 12 silf; & þat is riȝt meruelyous / I wole not leue for a litil to schewe a greet secreet, how ȝe may drawe out þe 5 beynge of ech of þe 4 elementis of al þe þing rehersid afore, and profitably

[* Fol. 18.]

Take any thing rotted and turned into water, as man's blood; put it in a glass distiller, and distil it over into an amphora.

schewe hem / And þe maner ys *þis / take þat þing putrified 16 and brouȝt into watir, what so euere ȝe wole, as I tauȝte ȝou tofore; and þat þing be mannes blood brouȝt into watir, of þe which ȝe wole drawe out þe 4 elementis / putte þerfore þat water, or þat blood putrified, in a stillatorie of glas, and sette 20 it wiþinne a pott of watir, and ȝeue vndirneþe a fier til þe watir of blood be distillid by þe pipe of þe lembike into a glas clepid

When no more vapour rises, you have drawn out the water.

amphora, riȝt clene / And whanne no þing may more by þat fier ascende, for certeyn ȝe haue of blood drawen out al oonly þe 24 element of watir / Forwhi. fier of þat bath hath no strenkþe to

Put the other 3 elements for 7 days into the same bath,

sublyme eyr, or fier, or erþe. and so [take] þo þre elementis, and sette in þe same bath by .vij. dayes þat þei be weel meyngid, & so cloos þat no þing be distillid / aftir þe .vij. dayes take þe 28

then into a coal fire, and the water shall rise as oil shining like gold,

stillatorie, and putte it to þe fier of aischen, þat is strongere þan fier of bath clepid marien; and þe watir schal ascende in foorme of oyle schynynge as gold / and aftirward þat no þing more schal ascende, ȝe haue þanne in þe ampulle .ij. elementis, þat is to seie, 32 watir and eyr. & oon from anoþir ȝe schal departe in þe bath,

the air remaining at the bottom like oil of gold. Put these aside.

puttynge yn aȝen wher al-oonly þe cleer watir schal ascende / and þe eyr schal al-oonly remayne iñ þe botum of þe vessel in lijknesse of oyle of gold. þe which oyle þat is gold, þe which oyle 36 þat is ayr / putte it aside. þanne þer leeueþ ʒitt fier wiþ erþe. to departe fier from erþe, putte þe element of watir, þat is to seye .iiij ℔ of watir, vpon j ℔ of mater / and putte by .vij. daies 4 to encorpere wel as tofore in þe bath of marien / Aftirward putte it to þe fier of flawme riʒt strong, and þe reed water schal ascende. þe which gadere togidere as longe as ony *þing ascendiþ. and to ʒou schal remayne an erþe riʒt blak in þe botum. þe which 8 gadere togidere aside / þanne þe redeste watir ʒe schal take. forwhy. þer be .ij. elementis, þat is to seie, þe element of watir and fier. þanne yn þe stillatorie, to þe fier of baþ, cleer watir schal asende. and in þe botum schal remayne þe reed watir, þat is, þe element 12 of fier. and so ʒe haue now first oon oyle, þat is, ayer o side, and watir, and fier, and erþe. and note ʒe weel þat þerfore þe element of watir is putt aʒen to drawe out from erþe fier and eyr, for þei wole not ascende, but þoruʒ þe help of element of watir. brynge 16 aʒen euerych into 5 beynge wiþ þe vessel of circulacioun as tofore / or ellis rectifie, makynge oon ascende .7 tymes bi an oþir / but first ʒe moste þe riʒt blak erþe of oon hide[1] nature, in þe furneys of glas mon[2], or ellis reuerberacioun, xxj. dayes calcyne / 20 And for a cause I speke to ʒou nomore of this science. but ioie ʒe, and thanke oure glorious lord god of þese þingis þat ʒe haue had.

The science to fixe alle erþely þingis in nostra 5ᵗᵃ essencia, 24 þat is to seie, oure heuene, þat by her influence þei may ʒeue þerto þer propertees and her hid vertues / oure glorious god haþ ʒeue sich a uertu to oure quinta essence, þat it may drawe out of euery matier of fruyʒt / tree / rote / flour, herbe / fleisch, 28 seed & spice / And euery medicynable þing, alle þe vertues, propirtees, and naturis, þe whiche god made in hem; and þat wiþinne .iij. houris.

Now I haue schewid ʒou a souereyn priuytee, how þat ʒe 32 may wiþ oure heuene drawe out euery 5 essencia from alle þingis aforeseid / þerfore alle necessarie þingis to euery syrup putte yn oure 5 essencie, & wiþinne .iij. houris þat watir schal be sich a sirup, vndirstonde wel, bettir by an hundrid part, by

¹ of vnkinde natuer. Harl. 853. ² of glasse made. Harl. 853.

[* Fol. 19.] *Whatever medicines are put into our Quinte Essence,*

cause of oure 5 essencie, þan it *schulde be wiþoute it / And so I seie of medicyns comfortatyues, digestyues, laxatyues, restriktyues, and alle oþere; forwhy. if ȝe putte seedis or flouris, fruyȝtis, leeues, spicis, coold, hoot, sweet, sour, moist, do þei good or yuel, into oure 5 essencie, forsoþe sich 5 essence ȝe schulen haue þerfore. oure 5 essencie is þe instrument of alle vertues of þing transmutable if þei be putt in it, encreessynge an hundrid foold her worchingis //

it increases their power a hundred fold.

4

8

End of Part I. **Explicit pars prima tractatus quinte essencie:**

BOOK II.

Here bigynneth the secunde book of medicyns / The first medicyn is to reduce an oold feble euangelik man to þe firste strenkþe of ȝongþe / Also to restore aȝen his nature þat is lost, and to lenkþe his lijf in greet gladnesse and perfiȝte heele vnto þe laste teerme of his lijf þat is sett of god / Ȝe schal take oure 5ta essencie aforeseid, þat is to seye, mannys heuene, and þerinne putte a litil quantite of 5 essencia of gold and of peerl. and þe oolde feble man schal vse þis deuyn drynk at morn and at euen, ech tyme a walnote-schelle fulle / and wiþinne a fewe dayes he schal so hool¹ þat he schal fele him silf of þe statt and þe strenkþe of xl ȝeer; and he schal haue greet ioie þat he is come to þe statt of ȝongþe. And whanne his ȝongþe is recouerid, and his nature restorid, and heelþe had, it is nedeful þat litil and seelde he vse 5 essence / Also it is nedeful þat he vse ofte good wiyn at his mete and at þe soper, in þe which be fixid þe 5. essence of gold, as I tauȝte ȝou tofore.

The secunde *medicyn is to heele a man, and make hym lyue, þat is almoost consumed in nature, and so nyȝ deed þat he is forsake of lechis. but if it be þe laste teerme of his lijf sett of god, ȝe schal ȝeue him oure quinte essence of gold wiþ a litil quantite of watir of celendoyn ȝdrawe, and meynge it wiþ þe oþere þingis aforeseid / and anoon as þe sike hath resceyued it into his stomak, it ȝeueþ to þe herte influence of naturel heete and of lijf. and þanne ȝe schal se him rise vp and speke, and wondirfully be comfortid and strenkþid þerby // þanne comforte him wiþ ministracioun of oure quinte essencie afore seid, and he schal be al hool / but if it be so þat god wole algatis þat he schal die / And I seie to ȝou truly, þat þis is þe hiȝeste maistrie þat may be in transmutacioun of kynde; for riȝt fewe lechis now lyuynge knowe þis priuytee.

¹ ? 'be so hool.' Or is *hool* a verb, become whole, recover?

HOW TO CURE LEPROSY AND PALSY. [Book II.

3a. Me.
To cure the Leprosy that is caused by rotten humours.

Use our Quinte Essence, with those of Gold and Pearl;

(or Burning Water, if you have no Quinte Essence.)

Wash the leper with strawberry or mulberry water; this is of great virtue,
[* Fol. 20.]
but is much encreased by our Quinte Essence.

4a. Me.
To cure Palsy, which comes from viscous humours closing the passages of motive power.

Blessed be God, our Quinte Essence will restore the paralitic.

Fix in it the Quinte Essence of euphorbium and the like; and, if God will, 'sawe'
the palsied man shall be whole, if you make him a stew of ivy
'Nota / yue / sauge.'
and sage.

Failing Quinte Essence, let him drink Burning Water

The þridde medicyn is to cure þe lepre þat is causid of corrupcioun and putrifaccioun of ony of þe principal humouris of man; but not þe lepre þat comeþ to man of kynde of þe fadir and of þe modir leprous,—for it is callid morbus 4 hereditus,—ne þe lepre þat is sent of god by his plage, but þat þat is causid oonly of rotun humouris / take oure 5 essence aforeseid, wiþ þe quinte essence of goold and peerl, a litil quantite at oonys, and vse it in maner as I seide afore / and wiþinne a 8 fewe daies he schal be partily hool þerof. and if ȝe haue non preparate redy oure 5 essence, þanne take in þe stide þerof fyn brennynge watir / but þat oþer is bettere.

Also, drawe a water of þe fruyȝt of strawbery or mulbery 12 tree, whanne it is ripe, and waische þe lepre þerwiþ. þis watir is of so greet vertu; for a souereyn maistir took it a leprous *womman, þat wiþ þe waischinge oonly of þis watir, withynne schort tyme was maad al hool / but sikirly þe vertu þerof is 16 myche worth if it be meyngid with oure 5 essence, or ellis brennynge watir; and þanne it schal be no nede to vse in þis perilous cure, venemys, as summe lechis doon.

The 4 medicyn is to cure palsie vniuersel. Forsoþe alle 20 philosophoris seyn þat þe palesye vniuersel comeþ of haboundaunce of viscous humouris closynge þe metis of vertu animale, sensityue, and motyue. And þerfore it is necessarie þat þo þingis þat schal cure þis sijknes be temperate, hoot, and moist, 24 and a litil attractyue, and to þe synous confortatyue / Therfore, blessid be god, makere of kynde, þat ordeynede for þe man paralitike oure 5 essence aforseid, þat souereynly to him comfortynge, restorynge, and temperatly worchynge / þerfore fixe 28 þerinne þe 5 essence of þo laxatyues þat purgen flewme & viscous humouris, as a litil of euforbie, or turbit, or sambucy. & þanne wiþoute doute, if god wole, þe paralitik man schal be hool wiþ comfortynge and restorynge of kynde, if ȝe make him 32 a stewe hoot and moist with herbis, þat is to seye, eerbe yue, & sauge, þat haue an heuenly strenkþe to comforte þe joynctis, & þe senewis, and þe vertu motyue. and if ȝe haue not redi preparate oure 5 essence, þanne take fyn brennynge watir til it 36

BOOK II.] TO CURE CONSUMPTION AND DRIVE AWAY DEVILS. 17

be redy, and lete þe pacient drynke þerof a litil in fyn wiyn. *in fine wine,*
and also he schal waische al his body and his extremytees wiþ *and wash all over with burning*
brennynge watir ofte tymes. and lete him vse þis a good while, *water.*
4 & he schal be hool. /
  The .5 medicyn for a man þat is almoost al consumed, [Fol. 20b.]
& waastid in al his body, and riȝt leene, as þat man þat   '5. Me.'
hath þe tisik & þe etik / Forsoþe þe verry cure to heele him *To fatten lean and consumptive*
8 is oure 5 essence / Forwhi. it comfortiþ þe feble nature; and *men.*
þe nature þat is lost it restoriþ, & so restorid it preserueþ / *Mix with our Quinte Essence*
And þerfore if ȝe wol restore þe fleisch of a leene mannys body
almoost consumed awey, drawe þanne a watir of celidoyne, and *'Celidoyne.'*
12 take þerof a litil quantite, and meynge wiþ oure 5 essence if ȝe *a little celandine water;*
haue it redy, or brennynge watir in stide þerof, and ȝeue it him *give it the patient, and*
to drinke; and wiþinne fewe dayes he schal be wondirfully *he shall soon be wonderfully fat.*
restorid and fat.
16 The .6. medicyn for passiouns of frenesie, foly, ymagyna- *'.6. Mo.'*
ciouns and noyous vexaciouns of deuelis, and also for þe *To cure Frensy, Gout, and*
goute als weel hoot as coold. certeyn experience techiþ þat *troubles from Devils.*
colerik men ȝeueþ to summe ymagynaciouns; and sangueyn *'colerike.' 'Sangueyn.'*
20 men ben ocupied aboute summe opere ymagynaciouns; & ȝitt *'Fleumatyke.'*
flewmatik men aboute opere / but þo men þat habounde in blak *'blake coler,' 'malencoly.'*
coler, þat is, malencoly, ben occupied a þousand part wiþ mo *Dark melancholy men are*
þouȝtis þan ben men of ony oþer complexioun / Forwhi. þat *troubled more with anxieties than any*
24 humour of blak coler is so noyous, þat if it a-bounde and a-sende *others,*
vp to þe heed, it troubliþ alle þe myȝtis of þe brayn, engendrynge
noyous ymagynaciouns, bryngynge yn horrible þouȝtis boþe *'Nota sequentia.'*
wakynge and slepinge; and siche maner of men ben born vndir *being born under 'Saturne, a wykyd*
28 þe constillacioun of saturne, the wickide planete / Forsoþe, to *turne, a wykyd planete.'*
siche men deuelis wole gladly appere, & minister to hem* her *[* MS. hom] Devils gladly*
priuy temptaciouns wiþinne þe cours of her þouȝtis; and þese *appear to them and*
men þus *turmentid wiþ þe passiouns of malencoly comounly *tempt them, [* Fol. 21.]*
32 speke wiþ hem, stryue and dispute wiþ hem silf whanne þei be
a-loone, þat ofte tymes opere folk may heere it / These maner *so that they often fall into*
of men þat ben þus turmentid, as weel by passioun of malencoly *despair and kill them-*
as of deuelis, ofte tymes falle in dispeir, and at þe laste sle hem *selves.*
36 silf / þe perfiȝt cure of alle þese is oure 5 essencie auri et *The cure is our Quinte*
  QUINTE ESSENCE.

perelar*um*, or ellis brennynge watir in stide þerof, in þe whiche ȝe fixe gold as it is aforeseid, wheri*n*ne be putt a litil of señē or watir of f[u]*miter*, or poudre of lapis lasuly, or ellis medulla*m* ebuli, and vse it discreetly. forwhy. not al oonly oure q*ui*nte essence auri *et* perelar*um* heelith þese disesis. / but also brennynge watir in þe which gold is fixid, heeliþ hem, wiþ a litil of þo þingis þat purgen and casten out blak coler supe*r*flue, & heliþ þe splene.

Forsoþe þese medicyns puttiþ awey wickid þouȝtis and an heuy herte malencolious; þei gladith and clense þe brayn and alle hise myȝtis, and brynge yn gladnes and merye þouȝtis. þei putte awey also þe craft of þe feendis temptac*i*ou*n*s, and ymagynaciouns of dispeir. þei distroie, & make a man to forȝete almaner of yueles, and naturaly bryngiþ him aȝen to resonable witt. and for as myche as saturne þe planete naturaly ys coold and drye, and is enemye to al kynde / Forwhy, euery snow, euery hayl, euery tempest, & also þe humour of malencoly comeþ of hi*m*. & he haþ his influence vpon derk leed, & vpon derk *placis vnder þe erf[1], foule and stynkynge, and derke wodis, and vpon foule, horrible, solitarie placis, as it is p*r*eued in vitas patru*m*, þat is to seye, in lyues & colac*i*ou*n*s of fadris / And also þe moone, naturely coold and moist, haþ his influence vpon þe nyȝt, and vpon myche moisture, and vpon þe placis whanne 4. weyes metiþ togidere. forsoþe in alle siche placis þei wole a-bide and schewe hem to her foloweris / but forsoþe þo þingis þat ben of þe nature of Iubiter and of sol, goode planetis, arne displesynge to hi*m*, and contrarie, and naturaly deuelis fle awei fro he*m*, for þei haue greet abhominaciou*n* of þer v*er*tuous influence / þerfore it schewiþ weel þat þo þingis þat ben in þis world, su*m*me þer ben þat bitokene þe glorious yoie of heuene, and su*m*me þing þat figure þe derknesse of euerlastynge peynes of helle / Forsoþe þe su*n*ne and iubiter, goode planetis, & gold, pure metal, and alle pure þingis þat gladen a man, figurynge by resou*n* þe ioie of heuene / and blak Saturne, and þe spotty moone, figure & bitokene þe condiciou*n* of helle / and

---

[1] Erf = erþe.

siþ þat deuelis be dampned, & ful of wreche of helle, þerfore
þei hate þe clennesse & þe ioie of oure lord god & of hise
seyntis / also þei haten þe sunne and his cleernes, and pure
þingis þat maken a man glad. and naturaly it plesiþ hem to
dwelle in derk, & in blak, orrible, stynkynge placis, in heuynesse, wreche, & malencoly, & in þo þingis þat pretende þe
condicioun of helle / And siþ oure 5. essence aforeseid is so
heuenly a þing, & by sotil craft *brouȝt to so myche swetnes,
it is so souereyn a medicyn þat it may weel be lijkned to þe ioie
of paradice. forwhi, it makiþ a man liȝt, iocunde, glad, and
merie, & puttiþ awey heuynesse[1], angre, melencoly, & wrapþe,
þe wluche þat deuelis loue / **et ideo nostra 5 essencia digne
vocatur celum humanum** / Also if a man be traueylid wiþ a
feend, and may not be delyuerid fro him, lete him drinke a litil
quantite of oure 5 essence, wiþ 5 essence of gold & peerl, and
wiþ an eerbe callid ypericon, i.[e.] fuga demonum, and þe seed
þerof grounden & aftirward distillid, & þe watir þerof a litil
quantite medlid wiþ þe oþere 5ᵗⁱˢ essenciis; *and* anoon þe deuel
wole fle awey fro him & fro his hous.

Also for þe goute, hoot or cold, þe pacient' schal drynke
oure 5. essence wiþ a litil quantite at oonys of þe letuarie de
succo rosarum. and lete him vse þis letuarie a litil at oonys ech
oþere day, til superflue humouris be purgid / but he schal vse
euery day a litil of oure 5. essence with 5 essence of gold &
peerle; & wiþinne a fewe dayes þe pacient schal be hool. //

The .7. medicyn, for to heele yche, & for to distrie lies[2]
þat ben engendrid of corrupt humouris. take oure 5 essence
bi him silf a-loone, and vse to drynke þerof a litil quantite
at oonys / and take also a litil quantite of Mer[curie?]. &
mortifie it wiþ fastynge spotil, & medle it wiþ a good quantite

---

[1] houynesse MS.

[2] "A lous is a worme with manye fete, & it commeth out of the filthi and onclene skynne, & oftentymes for faute of atendaunce they come out of the flesshe through the skynne or swet holes.

To withdryue them / The best is for to wasshe the oftentimes, and to chaunge oftentymes clene lynen."—*The noble lyfe and nature of man, Of bestes, serpentys, fowles, and fisshes* yᵗ *be moste knowen.* Capitulo. C. xix.

Marginal notes	Main text
Stavesacre and Burning Water. Wash the body or head where the itch and lice are. [* Fol. 22b.]	of poudre of stafi-sagre, & þanne put it in to a greet quantite of brennynge water, & þanne waische al his body, or ellis þe heed where þe icche & þe lies ben. & vse þis medicyn .2. or 3. & þe sijk *man schal be hool. 4
'.8ua. Me.' 'feuer quarteue.' To cure Quartan Fever.	The .8. medicyn for to cure 'the quarteyn and alle þe passiouns þat comeþ of malencoly in mannys body; and þe maistrie to purge malencoly. and ȝe schal vndirstonde þat þe quarteyn is gendrid of myche haboundaunce of malencolye þat 8
'ye quarten is ingendyrd of Malyncoly.' The Quartan arises from too much black choler, and lasts a year or more. To cure it soon, [*? our] drink our Quinte Essence;	is corrumpid withynne þe body. and for þis humour is erþely, coold, & drie, of þe nature of slowe saturne, þerfore þe accesse of þis sijknes ben slowe, and it duriþ comounly yn a man a ȝeer or more, and it puttiþ fro him gladnesse, & bryngiþ yn heuynes 12 more þan oþere feueris do / If ȝe wole heele þis sijknes in schort tyme, lete þe pacient vse to drynke oon* 5 essence, and he schal be al hool hastily / forwhi; it consumeþ þe corrupt superflue humouris, & reducit nature to equalite, and bryngiþ yn glad- 16
if you have it not, put pith of white dwarf elder in Burning Water, and take a walnut-shell full morning and evening.	nesse, & chasiþ a-wey heuynes & malencolie. and if it so be þat ȝe haue nouȝt oure 5 essence / þanne take j ℔ of þe beste brennynge watir, and þerinne putte medullam ebuli, and namely þe white, if ȝe may may haue it / of þis watir ȝeue to þe pacient, 20 morowe and euen, a walnot-schelle ful at oonys. and he schal
Or, take whatever purges black choler, put it into Burning Water; make small pellets of it, and take one, and then two, gradually.	be al hool / or ellis þus: take what þing ȝe wole þat purgiþ malencolye, and putte a litil þerof into brennynge watir, & vse þat laxatif maad into smale pelotis, wijsly resceyuyng riȝt a 24 litil at oonys, as oon litil pelot, and preue þerby how it worchiþ, þanne anoþer tyme .ij. at oonys, if it be nede / so þat þe mater be a litil digestid and a litil egestid. for bettere it is to worche a litil & a litil at oonys, þan sodeynly greue þe nature. forwhi, 28
[* Fol. 23.]	two litil pelotis laxatif meyngid wiþ brennynge watir *wole worche more myȝtily þan .8. pelotis wole do bi hem silf /
'Nota for ye quartene.' It is said that a tooth from a live beast heals the Quartan, and the juice of Hen-bit or Chickweed put in a man's nostrils.	Also philosophoris seyn þat a tooþ drawe out from a quyk beest, born vpon a man, delyueriþ fro þe quarteyn / Also 32 þei seyn þat if þe yuis of þe eerbe þat is callid morsus galline rubri be putt in hise nose-þrillis whanne he bigynneth to suffre þe accesse of þe quarteyn, he schal be hool, wiþ þe grace of god. 36

To cure Continual, Tertian, and Daily Fevers.

The medicyn to heele þe feuere contynuele. alle philosophoris seyn þat þe feuere contynuele is gendrid of putrifaccioun of blood and of corrupcieun of humouris in it / þerfore þe cure þerof is to purge blood, and to putte awey þe corrupcioun of it, & þe humoris vneuene to make euene, þe nature lost to restore, and so restorid to kepe / Forsoþe alle þese þingis worcheþ oure quinte essence; and þerfore it curiþ perfiȝtly þe feuere contynuele / and þouȝ brennynge watir caste out fro blood watry humouris and corrupt, ȝitt take it nouȝt in þis cure / forwhi; þouȝ brennynge watir be .7. tymes distillid, ȝitt it is [not] fully depurid fro his brennynge heete, & þe .4. elementis / but siþ oure 5. essence is not hoot, ne moist, coold, ne drie, as ben þe 4. elementis / þerfore it heeliþ perfiȝtly þe contynuel feuere; namely wiþ commixtioun of þe 5 essence of gold & peerle / and if ȝe wole strenkþe ȝoure medicyn, þanne putte yn oure 5. essence a litil quantite of pulpa cassie fistule / or ellis þe iuys of þe eerbe mercuriale. & if it so be þat oþere humouris habounde to myche with blood, þanne take þo laxatyues þat kyndely wole *purge hem, as comoun bookis of fisik declareþ.

The 10. medicyn to cure þe feuere tercian, þe which is causid of putrifaccioun, or reed coler to myche haboundynge / to cure þees sijknes, tak oure 5 essence, or ellis fyn brennynge watir,—but þe firste is bettere,—and putte þerinne a litil of rubarbe or of summe oþer laxatiue þat purgiþ reed coler, and a greet quantite of watir of endyue; and vse þis medicyn at morowe & euen. and þe pacient schal be hool wiþoute doute.

The 11. medicyn is for to heele þe feuere cotidian, þe which is causid of putrifaccioun of flewme to haboundynge / and siþ flewme is coold and moist. oure 5 essence (and in his absence take good brennynge watir.) haþ strenkþe and vertu to consume þe rotun watery inordinat, and to myche coold humidite / þerfore take oure 5 essence or brennynge watir, and putte þerinne a litil of euforbij, turbit, or sambuci, or sum oþir þing þat purgiþ flewme; and vse it morowe and eue, & þe pacient schal be hool.

'9ª. Mᵉ.'
To cure continual Fever.
It arises from putrefaction of blood and corruptions of humours.

Our Quinte Essence cures this, (tho' Burning Water does not,)

if mixed with Quinte Essence of Gold and Pearl,

and a little Cassia or Herb Mercury.

[* Fol. 23b.]

'10. Mᵉ.'
'feuer tercyane.'
To cure Tertian Fever.
Take Quinte Essence, with Rhubarb and Endive water, morn and eve.
'water of endyue.'

'.11. Mᵉ.'
'feuer cotydyan.'
To cure Daily Fever.
Take our Quinte Essence, and a little Euphorbium, &c.

22 TO CURE AGUE FEVER, LUNACY, AND CRAMP. [Book II.

'.12. Me.'
'lunatyke persons.'
To cure Ague Fever and Lunacy.
This fever comes of choler inflamed,

and is accompanied by lightheadedness.
'Nota bene.'

[* Fol. 24.]
'Signa.'
As the patient sees black, gold, or red things, so the different humours are inflamed.

Burning Water should not be taken,

but Quinte Essence of Gold and Pearl should, with that of Rose water, Violet, &c.

' for ye frenesye & wodnesse.'
To cure or asswage Frenzy and Madness.

Wrap the head and feet in, and smell at, Popilion (with Vinegar mixed), and Rue.

'13ª. Me.'
To cure Cramp.
Use our Quinte Essence or Burning Water.

The .12. medicyn for to cure þe feuere agu, and þe lunatik man and womman / discreet maistris seyn, þat þe feuere agu comounly is causid of a uyolent reed coler adust, and of blood adust, and of blak coler adust; and sumtyme of oon of 4 þese adust, and sumtyme of two togidere, and sumtyme of .3. togidere / and þerfore þe feuere agu is þe posityue degree, and in þe superlatyue degree, comparatif gree & superlatif gree / For þe feuere agu haþ comounly alienacioun of witt, & schew- 8 ynge of þingis of fantasy / And ȝe schal knowe weel whiche ben þe humouris adust þat causen þe feuere, be þese *tokenes / Forwhi, if þe pacient seiþ þat he seeþ blak þingis, þanne blak coler, þat is, malencolie, is adust / & if he se þingis of gold / 12 reed coler is adust / if reed þingis, and schewynge of bloodt þanne blood is adust / And if he seiþ þat he seeþ alle þese .iij, þingis, þanne alle þe humouris ben adust / For as myche as brennynge watir ascendiþ to þe heed, and gladly wole a man 16 drynke / And siþ þat feuere agu regneþ in þe regioun of þe heed / þe philosophoris counceilis þat þe pacient schal not resceyue it in þis sijknes / but it is nedeful þat he take oure 5 essence of gold and of peerl, meynging þe 6 part of 20 5 essence of watir of rose, violet, borage, and letuse[1] / and þanne ȝe schulen haue an heuenly medicyn to cure perfiȝtly þis sijknesse.   [[1] *in margin*, 'Rose / violett / Borage / lutuse /']

For to cure þe frenesye and woodnes, or ellis at þe leeste 24 to swage it / take a greet quantite of popilion, and þe beste vynegre þat ȝe may haue, and a good quantite of rewe domestik, weel brayed, and meyngid wiþ þese forseid þingis; and biclippe þe heed and þe feet of þe pacient with þis medicyn; and sum 28 þerof putte to his nose-þrillis. þis medicyn anoon puttiþ awey þe frenesye & þe schewynge of fantasies / it curiþ also wode men & lunatike men. and it restoriþ aȝen witt and discrecioun, & makiþ al hool and weel at eese.   32

The .13. medicyn is to put a-wey þe craumpe fro a man. for as myche as wise men seyn þat þe craumpe cometh of þe hurtynge & þe febilnes of þe senewis, as it schewiþ sumtyme yn medicyns maad of elebore, þer is no þing þat puttiþ awey þe 36

BOOK II.] TO CURE POISON AND COWARDICE. 23

craumpe as doiþ oure 5 essence aforeseid, or ellis *brennynge [* Fol. 24b.]
watir in stede of it.

The .14. medicyn, to caste out venym fro mannys body / '14ª. Mᵉ.'
4 take oure 5 essence, and putte þerine fleisch of a cok, neysch *To cast poison out of a*
soden & sotilly brayed, note kirnelis, fyn triacle, radisch, *man's body.*
& garleek smal brayed, and oþere þingis þat ben goode Take our Quinte Essence, with
to caste out venym, as comoun bookis of fisik declariþ / cock's flesh, nut-kernels,
8 And also, to comforte þe herte, putte yn oure foreseid 5. essence, &c., and Quinte Essence of Gold
þe 5. essence of gold and of peerl. and he schal be delyuerid and Pearls.
þerof & be hool.

The .15. medicyn, to make a man þat is a coward, hardy '15ª. Mᵉ.'
12 and strong, and putte a-wey almaner of cowardise and drede / *To make a Coward bold and strong.*
I seye ȝou forsoþe þat no þing may telle alle þe myraclis vertues þat god haþ maad in oure 5 essence, and not al oonly in
him, but also in to his modir, þat is to seye, fyn brennynge Give him our Quinte Essence with
16 watir. for to cure þis sijknesse, take a litil quantite of oure 5 sence with twice as much
essence, & putte þerto double so myche of brennynge watir, Burning Water, and a
and a litil quantite of þe iuys of eerbe pione and of saffron dis- little Peony juice and saffron, and
tillid togidere, and a litil of 5 essence of gold and of peerl; and Quinte Essence of Gold
20 ȝeue it him to drinke. and aftir sodeynly, as it were by myracle, and Pearl. The coward
þe coward man schal lese al maner drede and feyntnes of herte, shall lose all faintness of
and he schal recouere strenkþe þat ys lost by drede, and take to heart,
him hardynesse, and he schal dispise deeþ; he schal drede no
24 perelis, and passyngly he schal be maad hardy. þis is trewe, for
it haþ ofte tymes by oolde philosophoris [bene] preued / þerfore despise death, and dread no
it were a greet wisdom þat cristen princis, in bateilis aȝen perils. Therefore
heþene men, hadde wiþ hem in tonnes brennynge watir, þat Christian Princes
28 þei myȝt take to euery fiȝtynge man half a riȝt litil cuppe ful should have tuns of Burning Water,
þerof to drynke in þe bigynnynge of þe batel. & þis priuyte and give every fighting man
owith to be hid from alle enemyes of þe chirche; and also a cup before battle with
*princis and lordis ministringe þese þingis schulde not telle the heathen.
32 what it is. [* Fol. 25.]

The .16. medicyn aȝens þe feuere pestilenciale, and þe '16ª. Mᵉ.'
maistrie to cure it. forsoþe holy scripture seiþ þat summe *To cure Pestilential Fever*
tymes oure lord god sendiþ pestilence to sle summe maner *(when not sent as a punish-*
36 of peple, as it is seid deutronomium 28 in þis maner " Si *ment by God).*

24 TO CURE PESTILENTIAL FEVER AND PLAGUES. [BOOK II.

God says in Deuteronomy xxviii. that if men will not hear His voice and obey His commandments, pestilences shall come on them.

audire nolueris[1] vocem domini dei tui, ut custodias et facias omnia mandata eius, veniant super te omnes maledicciones; iste maledictus eris in ciuitate &c." et infra; "ad-iungat tibi pestilenciam donec consumat te de terra, percuciat te dominus egestate, febre, et frigore, ardore et estu, et aere corrupto ac rubigine, et persequatur donec pereas" hec ibidem; et infra "percuciat te dominus vlcere egipti, et partem corporis per quam stercora egerantur. scabie quoque, et prurigine, ita ut curari nequeas; percuciat te dominus necessitate ac furore mentis" //

These plagues a man would be a great fool to presume to cure,

Therfore a gret fool were he þat wolde presume to cure þese plagis of pestilence þat ben vncurable, þat ben sent of god to ponysche synne // Also 3e schal vndirstonde þat men may die in .iij. maners. in oon maner by naturel deeþ, in þe teerme þat is sett of god / In anoþir maner bi violent deeþ, and also in þe .iij. maner occasionaly wiþinne þe teerme þat is sett of god; as þo men þat to myche replecioun, or to greet abstynence or by disperacioun, or

but all other pestilences

ellis by necligence, sle him silf / but sikirly alle oþere maner of feueris pestilence þat god suffriþ to come to mankynde by

from evil planets may be cured by our Quinte 'Nota bene.' Essence with Aloes, Euphorbium, &c., [Fol. 25b.]*

perilous influence of yuele planetis, by þe grace of god & good gouernaunce may be curid partialy wiþ oure 5. essence. and þerinne putte a litil of aloes epatik & euforbij, & a litil of ierapigra galieni & of 5 essence, of þe rote of lilie and also of gold & peerle, capilli veneris *and ysope; for þese þingis ben nedeful to siche feueris & apostemes / it is nedeful also

and a laxative Quinte Essence that will send the patient to stool once a day.

þat wiþ þese þingis þer be sich a quinta essencia laxatyue þat wole purge þe superflue humouris þat abounde; and þat þe pacient so myche resceyue in a natural day þerof þat he may go weel oonys to sege; and so lete him vse þis laxatif .3. in þe woke; But be weel war þat he take wiþ oure quinta essencia

'Caueas.'

but riȝt a litil quantite of þe laxatif at oonys, as I tolde ȝou

He must also take every morning an egg-shell-full of Burning Water, and 2 or 3 pestilence pills in our Quinte Essence, and smoke his

tofore, for peril þat miȝte bifalle. & euery day take he by þe morowe an eye-schelle ful of good brennynge watir, and þe corrupt eyr schal not noye him; & also vse in þe dayes, two or þre smale pelotis pestilenciales in oure 5 essencia, or in brennynge watir; & al þe hous of þe pacient schal be encensid

4

8

12

16

20

24

28

32

[1] MS. volueris.

BOOK II.] MAY THIS BOOK FALL INTO NO BAD MAN'S HANDS! 25

strongly .iij in þe day wiþ frank-encense, mirre, & rosyn, *house with frankincense, &c.*
terbentyn & rewe. and þis is perfiȝt cure for þe feuere pesti-
lence / And þus ȝe may, wiþ þis 5 essencijs, cure alle þese sijk-
4 nesses aforeseid, and manye oþere, as it were by myracle, if ȝe
worche disc[r]cetly as I haue toold ȝou tofore / Now here *Here is an end of this most sovereign of all secrets.*
I make an eende of þis tretis þat is clepid þe mooste & þe
souereyneste secrete of alle secretis, and a passynge tresour
8 þat may nouȝt fayle // O quantum malum foret, si hic *What ills will befall if it gets into tyrants' and reprobates' hands and prolongs their life in evil. I will keep it for holy men alone; and I commend it to Christ's keeping now and ever.*
liber perueniret ad manus hominum mundanorum, ad noticiam
tirannorum, et ad seruicium reproborum! quia, sicut sancti per
hunc librum poterunt continuare opera vite christiani diucius
12 et vehemencius, ita et reprobi possent peruerso vsi diucius
perseuerare in malo. ego autem, quantum in me est, propter
solos sanctos librum hunc constituo, et ipsum custod[iæ] ihesu
Christi commendo nunc et in eternum // = //

16 **Explicit librum de maximis secretis essencie quinte &c.**

THE SPHERES AND PLANETS. [leaf 26]

¶ Philosofirs puttyn 9 sper*is* vndirewritten; but Diuinis puttin þe tenþe spere, where is heuyn empire, in þe whiche, angel*is* & sowl*is*[1] of seynt*is* seruen god; i*n* þe whiche is crist, in þe same forme that he walkid i*n* erþe, and also owr*e* lady, & seynt*is* that arosen wit*h* criste.

¶ þe first spere of þe 9 is clepid ʻ pr*i*mum mobile,' þe first mevabil thyng.

¶ þe .ij. spere of sterr*is* : Aries .1. þe rame. ¶ the secund hows of Mars, þe bool, ¶ þe secund hows of Venus, Gemini, ¶ þe secund hows of Mercuri, Cancer. ¶ þe hows of þe mone, leo. þe hows of þe sonne, Virgo. // þe first hows of Mercury, Libra // þe first hows of Venus, Scorpio // þe first hows of Mars, Sagittari*us* // þe first hows of Iubit*er*, Cap*ri*cornus // þe first hows of Saturne, Aquari*us* // þe secund hows of Saturne, Piscis./ þe secunde hows of Iubit*er* [*no more*].

¶ Saturn is a planete evel-willid and ful of sekenes. Wherfore he is peyntid wit*h* an hooke, for he repeþ down) grene thyng*is* / he fulfilliþ his course in xxx ʒeere.

¶ Iubit*er* is a planete wele willyng to alle thing*is* to be gendrid, plent[i]ful & plesyng; therfor he is y-seid Iubit*er* as helpyn. i*n* xij [ʒ]eere he filliþ his course.

¶ Mars is an enemy to alle thyng*is* to be gendrid ; wherfor he is clepid god of batel, for he is ful of tempest. he fulfilliþ his course i*n* .ij. ʒeere. [leaf 26, back]

¶ þe sonne is þe worthiest planet, y-set i*n* myddis. he fulfilliþ his course in CCClxv dayes & vj. howr*is*, þe whiche causen bisext.

¶ Venus is apte to alle thyng*is* to be gendrid. he fulfilliþ his course in CCCxxxvj daies.

¶ Mercuri swyft is y-seid a messeng*er* of daies [? heuene]. he fulfilliþ his course i*n* CCCxxxvj daies.

¶ þe mone is a planete ny þe erþe. [*ends.*]

[1] l*is* is the MS. l with a line at right angles to it.

NOTES

ON THE CHEMISTRY OF THE TEXT

BY C. H. GILL, ESQ., OF UNIVERSITY COLLEGE, LONDON

P. 4. Direction to submit any wine *that is not sour* to distillation. (*Sour* wine is deficient in alcohol; that body having been changed into acetic acid by oxidation.) In the language of the mystical ideas which prevailed in the dawn of Chemistry, the colouring matters, sugar, &c. of the wine are called 'the .4. elementis,' or as it were the 'rotten fæces of wine'??

The direction to distill the wine seven times is a good practical suggestion for the obtaining of strong alcohol which will burn well. Then follows a description of the distilling apparatus, which seems to have been arranged to ensure a very slow distillation, so as to obtain a product as colourless and scentless as possible.

P. 5. The second way to make the Quinte essence depends on distillation of alcohol by means of the heat of fermenting horse-dung; also the fifth manner.

P. 6. The directions for gilding burning water are all nonsense; but as the writer had no means of testing the truth of his statements, they may have been made in good faith.

P. 7. The idea which he expresses, that this gilt burning water will make you well and young, is difficult to explain, except on the assumption that, it being the strongest of alcohol, a very little served to produce that elevation of spirits which seemed to bring back the spring of youth.

P. 7, l. 6 from the bottom. The word *liquibles* in the text does not mean liquids, for a liquid cannot be made hot enough to be *quenched*. If the original *liquibles* cannot be retained I should substitute the word *liquiables*, meaning those things which can be liquefied by heat. Indeed in the next passage we find stated that if Saturn (the alchemists' mystical name for Lead) be quenched, &c., and that if then Mars (Iron) be quenched in the same liquid, it will acquire the softness of Saturn. Or if you quench lead in spirit which has had iron first cooled in it, it becomes hard.

Of course there is no truth whatever in the above statements.

P. 8. The fire without coals, &c., is 'corrosive sublimate,' most probably containing an excess of Sulphuric acid (vitriol) as an impurity. If Copper (Venus) or Tin (Jupiter) be dipt into this solution of mercury they will have a deposit of mercury formed on their surface, which will give them a pearly appearance.

P. 8. To bring Gold into calx. When gold is treated in the way directed, a fine powder of gold of a brown or yellow colour is left. This might readily have been mistaken for a calx by those who had no clear ideas of what calx really was.

P. 9. The departing of gold from silver is essentially the same as the plan practised at the present day.

To get the Quintessence of Gold. I can make nothing of the directions, that is, I cannot see that they (the directions) hide any real truth.

P. 10. How to get the Quintessence of Antimony. I can make nothing of this part, and can only suggest that the vinegar used contained hydrochloric acid, and when distilled with 'Myn Antimony' (native sulphide of antimony) gave a distillate of Chloride of Antimony containing some 'kermes' which is red.

From this point onward there is little or nothing that can be explained by a Chemist.

GLOSSARY.

Agu, p. 22, l. 1, 'Intermittent Feaver, commonly called an *Ague*, has certain times of Intermission or ceasing; it begins for the most part with Cold or Shivering, ends in Heat, and returns exactly at set Periods.' *Phillips*.

Aischin, p. 4, l. 10, ashes.

Amphora, p. 11, &c., 'a large vessel which derived its name from its being made with a handle on each side of the neck, from ἀμφί *on both sides*, and φέρω *I carry*.' *Dict. of Gr. and Rom. Ant.*

Anele, p. 6, l. 26, &c., heat?

Apostemes, p. 24, l. 24, imposthumes, boils.

Appeire, p. 3, l. 12, impair, worsen.

Arreins, p. 2, l. 25, spiders.

'Cassia Fistula (Lat.), [p. 21, l. 16], Cassia in the Pipe or Cane, a kind of Reed or Shrub that grows in *India* and *Africa*, bearing black, round, and long Cods, in which is contain'd a soft black Substance, sweet like Honey, and of a purging Quality.' *Phillips*.

Colaciouns, p. 18, l. 21, ? comments, homilies.

Comounne, p. 3, l. 35, communicate.

'Continual Feaver [p. 21] is that whose Fit is continu'd for many Days; having its times of Abatement, and of more Fierceness; altho' it never intermits, or leaves off.' *Phillips*.

Deedly, p. 3, l. 24, liable to death, mortal.

Departynge, p. 5, l. 14, parting, separating.

Depurid, p. 9, l. 27, purified, purged.

Distillatorie, p. 10, l. 24, a still. Randle Holme, (*Academy*, p. 422, col. 2,) speaks of a Still or Distillatory Instrument,' and further on, iv., 'He beareth Sable, the Head of a *Distillatory* with 3 pipes; having as many Receivers or Bottles set to them.'

'Ebulum or Ebulus (Lat.), [p. 18, l. 3] the Herb *Wall-wort, Dane-wort*, or *Dwarf-elder*.' *Phillips*.

Encorpere, p. 13, l. 4, mix, incorporate.

Euforbii, p. 21, l. 3 bot., 'Euphorbia, the *Libyan Ferula*, a Tree or Shrub first found by King *Juba*, and so call'd from the Name of his Physician *Euphorbus*.' *Phillips*.

Euphorbium, 'the gummy Juice or Sap of that Tree much us'd in Physick and Surgery.' *Phillips*.

Extremities, p. 17, l. 2, ends of the limbs.

Fecis, p. 4, l. 7; p. 9, dregs.

Fire of hell, p. 8, l. 23, a disease.

Fumiter, p. 18, l. 3, fumitory.

Fyme, p. 10, l. 2 bot., mud, clay.

Gerapigra galieni, p. 3, l. 29, ἱερα πικρα Γαληνου.

GLOSSARY.

Giltid, p. 7, l. 3, having the properties of gold communicated by it.

Groste, p. 5, ll. 9, 29, grossness, heavy particles, residuum.

Hide, p. 13, l. 18, ? for hide*us*; compare the Harleian reading 'unkinde.'

Hool, p. 15, l. 10, recover, improve.

Incombustible, p. 10, l. 2.
Incorruptibility, p. 7, l. 2.

Kynde, p. 1, l. 12, all creatures; l. 13, nature.

'Lapis Lazuli [p. 18, l. 3] a kind of Azure or Sky-colour'd Stone, of which the Blew Colour call'd *Ultramarine* is made . . much us'd in Physick.' *Phillips.*

Lembike, p. 9, l. 2, 'Alembick or Limbeck (Arab.), a Still, a Chymical Vessel used in Distilling, shaped like a Helmet, and towards the Bottom having a Beak or Nose, about a Foot and a half long, by which the Vapours descend. They are commonly made of Copper tinn'd over on the inside, and often of Glass.' *Phillips.*

Liquibles, p. 7, l. 6 bot., meltable metals.

Lymayl, p. 8, l. 6 bot., Fr. '*limaille:* f. File-dust, pinne-dust.' *Cotgrave.*

Marien Bath, p. 12, l. 7 bot., Balneum Mariæ, a Chemist's bath. '*Bain de Marie.* Maries bath; a cauldron, or kettle full of hot water.' *Cotgrave.*

Medle, p. 19 last line, mix.

Medulla, p. 18, l. 3, pith.

Mercasite, p. 10, l. 14, 'a kind of Mineral Stone, hard and brittle, partaking of the Nature and Colour of the Metal it is mixed with; some call it a Fire-Stone.' *Phillips.*

Mercuriale, mercurie, p. 21, 19, &c., 'Mercury . . among Chymists . . signifies Quick-silver; and is also taken for one of their active Principles, commonly call'd *Spirit* . . Also the Name of a purging Herb, of which there are two sorts, *viz. Good Harry* and *Dog's Mercury.*'

Metis, p. 16, l. 22, *meatus*, passages.

Mon, p. 13, l. 19.?

Morsus Gallinæ, the Herb Henbit or Chick-weed. *Phillips.*

Mortifie, p. 19 last line, 'Among Chymists to change the outward Form or Shape of a Mixt Body; as when Quicksilver, or any other Metal, is dissolved in an *acid Menstruum.*' *Phillips.*

Neischede, p. 7, l. 2 bot., neshness, softness, pliancy.

Oo, p. 4, one.

Popilion, p. 22, l. 24; 'Populeum, an Ointment made of Poplar buds, of a cooling and allaying Quality.' *Phillips.* Fr. '*Populeon.* Popilion, a Pompillion; an ointment made of blacke Poplar buds.' *Cot.*

Preparate, p. 8, l. 21, prepare.

'Quartan Ague [p. 20] is that whose Fit returns every fourth Day.' *Phillips.*

Quenchour, p. 6 at foot, cooling the florin?

Quintessence is defined by Phillips as 'the purest Substance drawn out of any Natural Body; a Medicine made of the efficacious active Particles of its Ingredients separated from all *Fæces* or Dregs; the Spirit, chief Force, or Virtue of any thing.'

Reme, p. 9, l. 5 bot., A.S. *reoma*, a strap, thong.
Reparale, p. 8, l. 21, make, compound.
Respire, p. 4, l. 5 from foot, exhale.
Restreyne, p. 7, l. 8, retain.
Reward, p. 2, l. 4, 7, regard.
Rotombe, p. 10, l. 3 bot., a retort.

Sambucy, p. 16, l. 7 bot., 'Sambucus, the Elder-Tree; a Shrub of very great use in Physic.' *Phillips*.
Stafisagre, p. 20, l. 1, 'Staphis agria, the Herb Staves-acre, or Lice-bane.' *Phillips*.

'Tertian Ague or Feaver [p. 21] is that which intermits entirely, and returns again every third Day with its several Symptoms at a set Time.' *Phillips*.
To, p. 1, l. 16, too.

Triacle, p. 23, l. 5, cordial, 'Treacle, a Physical Composition, made of Vipers and other Ingredients.' *Phillips*.
Turbit, p. 16, l. 7 bot., 'Turbit, Tripoly, an Herb called Turbith, or blew Camomel.'
'Turbith, an Herb so call'd by the Arabians, which grows in Cambaya, Surat, and other parts of Asia; a dangerous Drug upon account of its violent purging Quality.' *Phillips*.

Vapoure, p. 8, l. 5 from foot; p. 9 at foot, evaporate.

Woodnes, p. 22, l. 23, wildness, madness.

Ypericon, p. 19, l. 16, 'Hypericon, St. *John's-Wort*, an excellent Herb for Wounds, and to provoke Urine.' *Phillips*.

The manufacturer's authorised representative in the EU for product safety is Oxford University Press España S.A. of El Parque Empresarial San Fernando de Henares, Avenida de Castilla, 2 - 28830 Madrid (www.oup.es/en or product.safety@oup.com). OUP España S.A. also acts as importer into Spain of products made by the manufacturer.
Printed and bound by CPI Group (UK) Ltd, Croydon, CR0 4YY

20/03/2026

02075341-0002